W9-BCY-491

Thinking Critically: Gun Control

John Allen

ReferencePoint Press®

San Diego, CA

© 2018 ReferencePoint Press, Inc.
Printed in the United States

For more information, contact:
ReferencePoint Press, Inc.
PO Box 27779
San Diego, CA 92198
www.ReferencePointPress.com

Picture Credits:
All charts and graphs by Maury Aaseng

LIBRARY OF CONGRESS CATALOGING-IN-PUBLICATION DATA

Name: Allen, John, 1957– author.
Title: Thinking Critically: Gun Control/by John Allen.
Description: San Diego: ReferencePoint Press, [2017] | Series: Thinking Critically | Audience:
   Grade 9 to 12.
Identifiers: LCCN 2017041159 (print) | LCCN 2017047495 (ebook) | ISBN 9781682823385 (eBook)
   | ISBN 9781682823378 (hardback)
Subjects: LCSH: Gun control—Juvenile literature.
Classification: LCC HV7435 (ebook) | LCC HV7435 .A445 2017 (print) | DDC 363.330973—dc23
LC record available at https://lccn.loc.gov/2017041159

Contents

Foreword

"Literacy is the most basic currency of the knowledge economy we're living in today." Barack Obama (at the time a senator from Illinois) spoke these words during a 2005 speech before the American Library Association. One question raised by this statement is: What does it mean to be a literate person in the twenty-first century?

E.D. Hirsch Jr., author of *Cultural Literacy: What Every American Needs to Know*, answers the question this way: "To be culturally literate is to possess the basic information needed to thrive in the modern world. The breadth of the information is great, extending over the major domains of human activity from sports to science."

But literacy in the twenty-first century goes beyond the accumulation of knowledge gained through study and experience and expanded over time. Now more than ever literacy requires the ability to sift through and evaluate vast amounts of information and, as the authors of the Common Core State Standards state, to "demonstrate the cogent reasoning and use of evidence that is essential to both private deliberation and responsible citizenship in a democratic republic."

The *Thinking Critically* series challenges students to become discerning readers, to think independently, and to engage and develop their skills as critical thinkers. Through a narrative-driven, pro/con format, the series introduces students to the complex issues that dominate public discourse—topics such as gun control and violence, social networking, and medical marijuana. Each chapter revolves around a single, pointed question such as Can Stronger Gun Control Measures Prevent Mass Shootings?, or Does Social Networking Benefit Society?, or Should Medical Marijuana Be Legalized? This inquiry-based approach introduces student researchers to core issues and concerns on a given topic. Each chapter includes one part that argues the affirmative and one part that argues the negative—all written by a single author. With the single-author format the predominant arguments for and against an

4

issue can be synthesized into clear, accessible discussions supported by details and evidence including relevant facts, direct quotes, current examples, and statistical illustrations. All volumes include focus questions to guide students as they read each pro/con discussion, a list of key facts, and an annotated list of related organizations and websites for conducting further research.

The authors of the Common Core State Standards have set out the particular qualities that a literate person in the twenty-first century must have. These include the ability to think independently, establish a base of knowledge across a wide range of subjects, engage in open-minded but discerning reading and listening, know how to use and evaluate evidence, and appreciate and understand diverse perspectives. The new *Thinking Critically* series supports these goals by providing a solid introduction to the study of pro/con issues.

Gun Control

Few incidents have encapsulated the debate over gun control in America like the one that occurred on the sunny spring morning of June 14, 2017. At a baseball field in Alexandria, Virginia, which is just outside Washington, DC, a man armed with a semiautomatic rifle opened fire on members of a Republican congressional baseball team practicing for the annual game with their Democrat rivals. The shooter wounded five people before US Capitol Police officers shot and killed him. House Majority Whip Steve Scalise of Louisiana suffered critical injuries in the attack and was rushed to a local hospital along with the other victims.

No sooner had the news hit the Internet and television networks than proponents began to raise familiar points of the gun debate. Supporters of gun rights insisted the incident could have been much worse had individuals with guns—in this case the US Capitol Police—not been there to stop the shooter. "Put it this way," said Rep. Chuck Fleischmann, a pro–gun rights Tennessee Republican who was at the field, "if we had had more weapons there, we could have subdued that shooter more quickly. Thank God that the Capitol Police were there and were armed, because otherwise we'd have had a situation where there'd been a lot more damage."[1] Gun control advocates focused on why the gunman was able to obtain a military-style

> "We're always hopeful that Congress will get with the program, do right by the American people and pass reform that keeps guns out of dangerous hands. It's what keeps us coming back every day."[2]
>
> —Dan Gross, president of the Brady Campaign to Prevent Gun Violence

weapon in the first place. "We're always hopeful that Congress will get with the program, do right by the American people and pass reform that keeps guns out of dangerous hands," said Dan Gross, president of the Brady Campaign to Prevent Gun Violence. "It's what keeps us coming back every day."[2]

A Culture of Gun Ownership

Mass shooting incidents have become all too common in modern America. In 2016 alone there were three high-profile shootings. In June a shooter with a semiautomatic rifle attacked patrons at a gay nightclub in Orlando, Florida, killing forty-nine and wounding fifty-eight. One month later an armed individual in Dallas, Texas, ambushed a group of police officers, killing five and injuring nine others. In December a gunman opened fire in a church in Charleston, South Carolina, murdering nine people, including the pastor. Following each attack, there arose a heated debate about gun control. Such debates are passionate but almost always lead nowhere. "Tragically, gun control has become one of those fact-free issues that spawn outbursts of emotional rhetoric and mutual recrimination about the National Rifle Association or the Second Amendment,"[3] says Thomas Sowell, an economist and writer on national affairs. Generally, those on the political left favor tougher gun laws and tighter restrictions on gun ownership, while those on the right support the opposite positions.

> "Tragically, gun control has become one of those fact-free issues that spawn outbursts of emotional rhetoric and mutual recrimination about the National Rifle Association or the Second Amendment."[3]
>
> —Thomas Sowell, American economist and writer on national affairs

Guns are a part of everyday life in America to an extent that many people outside the United States find hard to understand. According to the Pew Research Center, estimates of the number of guns in the United States range up to 310 million—which represents about one firearm for each person in the country. More than 35 percent of Americans either own a gun or live with someone who does. By contrast, the United Kingdom banned handguns in 1997 and restricts ownership of rifles and shotguns to hunters and members of shooting clubs. Australia also passed strict gun control laws more than two decades ago, banning the possession and sale of semiautomatic firearms and pump-action shotguns.

Foreign observers often equate the enormous number of guns in the United States with an overall culture of violence, as seen in American movies and TV dramas. America's gun culture dates to the first European settlers, who used guns to hunt for food, obtain pelts for the fur market, and protect against animal attacks. They also used guns against native peoples. The ability to shoot with accuracy was regarded as necessary for a young man leaving home to start a family. In the Revolutionary War, many colonists resorted to using their own firearms and ammunition in organizing militia units. Guns played a major role in westward expansion, from protecting wagon trains against bandits and hostile native tribes (who also wielded rifles) to enforcing the law in frontier towns. The cowboy with a holstered pistol on his hip became an emblem of the American West worldwide. With guns such a fundamental part of America's self-image, ownership of firearms continued even as cities and towns developed.

Reading the Second Amendment

Debates about America's gun culture often revolve around interpretations of the Second Amendment, which deals with firearms. Written by James Madison in 1789, the amendment reads as follows: "A well regulated Militia, being necessary to the security of a free State, the right of the people to keep and bear Arms, shall not be infringed."[4]

Although the Second Amendment consists of fewer than thirty words, its meaning has been the subject of endless debate. Gun control advocates say the intent of the amendment is to limit the possession of guns to members of a militia—that is, to organized military groups in the states. These advocates argue that the federal government or the states can restrict or outlaw gun ownership with regard to nonmilitia individuals. On the other hand, those in favor of gun rights focus on what they

Gun Laws Differ Dramatically from State to State

The United States has a patchwork of gun laws. While some states have many regulations, others have almost none. In a June 15, 2017, article, the *Washington Post* detailed its findings after looking into five types of gun control laws enacted by states. The five are: assault weapons bans; high-capacity magazine bans; gun possession prohibitions for high-risk individuals; gun possession prohibitions for individuals with domestic violence convictions; and mandatory background checks. The reporters found that six states (California, New York, New Jersey, Maryland, Massachusetts, and Connecticut) and the District of Columbia each had all five types of gun control laws. They found that two states (Idaho and Montana) had none of these laws.

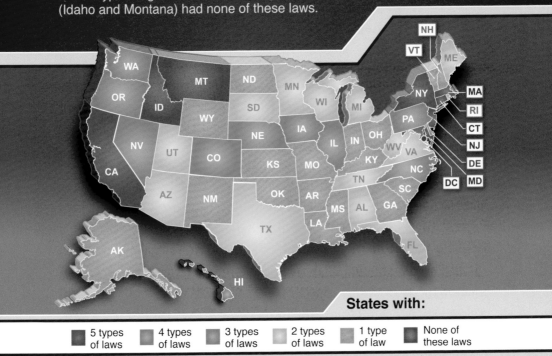

States with:

- 5 types of laws
- 4 types of laws
- 3 types of laws
- 2 types of laws
- 1 type of law
- None of these laws

Source: Leslie Shapiro, Sahil Chinoy, and Aaron Williams, "How Strictly Are Guns Regulated Where You Live?," *Washington Post*, June 15, 2017. www.washingtonpost.com.

see as the amendment's core statement, that the government shall not infringe on (or restrict) a citizen's right to keep and bear arms. Gun rights supporters read the initial clause about a militia as a suggestion that does not affect the basic right set out in the text.

For more than a century, the gun control viewpoint prevailed in the Supreme Court and the lower courts. For example, in *United States v. Miller* (1939), the court ruled that the Second Amendment did not protect the right to own and carry a firearm if there was not some reasonable connection to militia activity. As the *New Yorker's* legal analyst Jeffrey Toobin notes, "The courts had found that the first part [of the amendment], the 'militia clause,' trumped the second part, the 'bear arms' clause."[5] Although gun control as an issue brought spirited debate, Congress was still able to pass laws such as the Gun Control Act of 1968, which regulated interstate and foreign commerce in firearms.

The Brady Bill and the *Heller* Decision

In 1977 the National Rifle Association (NRA) began to stump for the rights of gun owners. Whereas the NRA previously had focused on non-controversial topics such as gun safety and sport shooting, the group's new leadership sought recognition of an individual's right to own and use firearms. The debate over gun control became more heated with passage of the Brady Handgun Violence Prevention Act in 1993. James Brady, who served as President Ronald Reagan's press secretary, was shot in the head during a lone gunman's assassination attempt on Reagan outside a hotel in Washington, DC, in 1981. The shooting left Brady with partial paralysis. Subsequently, Brady and his wife pushed for tougher gun laws through the Brady Campaign to Prevent Gun Violence. The Brady bill that finally passed set up a system of background checks and a five-day waiting period for those seeking to purchase firearms. Since its passage, according to US Department of Justice statistics, the law has blocked more than 2.4 million gun sales to felons and others who are ineligible to buy guns.

Laws seeking to outlaw gun ownership altogether have fared less well. In the 2008 case *District of Columbia v. Heller*, the Supreme Court affirmed the right of individuals to own a firearm. In his lead opinion, Justice Antonin Scalia rejected the Washington, DC, ban on handguns, noting that "handguns are the most popular weapon chosen by Americans for self-defense in the home, and a complete prohibition of their use is invalid."[6] Scalia acknowledged that the Second Amendment's opening clause about militias set out a purpose, but he believed that purpose could not limit "the right of the people"—meaning *all* people, not just militia members—to keep guns. Gun control advocates reacted with shock at what they saw as *Heller's* dangerously sweeping changes to traditional firearms laws. At the same time, the NRA declared victory in its campaign for individual gun rights.

An Ongoing Emotional Debate

Neither the Brady bill nor the *Heller* decision came anywhere close to ending America's gun debate. Following a deadly shooting that killed twenty children and six adults at Sandy Hook Elementary School on December 14, 2012, President Barack Obama reacted to the national outrage by calling for tougher gun laws. Obama issued an executive order that required more extensive criminal background checks on gun buyers and pushed for a ban on assault weapons and large gun magazines that hold more bullets. Yet Obama and his supporters failed to persuade Congress to pass new laws. Some conservatives declared that the president's strong push for gun control actually boosted gun sales among those fearful of widespread bans.

Strong voices on both sides of the gun debate are sounding again, this time in connection with two mass shootings in late 2017—one in October in Las Vegas, Nevada and the other in November in Sutherland Springs, Texas. In Las Vegas, at least fifty-eight people were killed and hundreds injured when a gunman on a high floor of a hotel rained a rapid-fire barrage on people below who were attending a three-day outdoor country music event. In Sutherland Springs, twenty-six people were killed and twenty injured when a gunman entered the First Baptist Church during worship services and opened fire with a semiautomatic rifle. Although the shootings were unrelated, in both cases the shooters used rapid-fire, assault-style weapons. Both shootings are likely to add to the long-running and always-emotional debate over gun rights and gun control in the United States.

Chapter One

Do Gun Control Laws Reduce Gun-Related Deaths?

Gun Control Laws Reduce Gun-Related Deaths

- Countries with strict gun control laws have significantly lower murder rates.
- If guns were not so easy to obtain, fewer criminals would use them to commit crimes.
- Gun control laws also help prevent suicides and accidental deaths from firearms.

The Debate at a Glance

Gun Control Laws Do Not Reduce Gun-Related Deaths

- Cities such as Washington, DC, and Chicago have strict gun control laws yet also have high murder rates.
- Criminals and terrorists will find a way to get guns despite the toughest gun control laws.
- Some countries, such as Switzerland, have high gun ownership rates and low homicide rates.

Gun Control Laws Reduce Gun-Related Deaths

"The more guns there are in a country, the more gun murders and massacres of children there will be. Even within this gun-crazy country, states with strong gun laws have fewer gun murders (and suicides and accidental killings) than states without them."

—Adam Gopnik, editorial writer for the *New Yorker*

Adam Gopnik, "The Simple Truth About Gun Control," *New Yorker*, December 20, 2012. www.newyorker.com.

Consider these questions as you read:

1. Which arguments in favor of expanding gun control laws do you find most persuasive—and why?
2. Do you believe that the gun culture in America can be changed? Should it be changed? Why or why not?
3. What effect do you think stronger gun control laws would have on suicide rates in the United States? Explain.

Editor's note: The discussion that follows presents common arguments made in support of this perspective, reinforced by facts, quotes, and examples taken from various sources.

Each time there is a mass shooting in the United States—and there always seems to be another occurrence—hopes are raised about sensible gun control. Supporters think surely this time Congress will at last rise above its partisan squabbles and pass the tougher gun control laws needed to stop the violence. Most citizens recognize the simple correlation between easy availability of guns and higher rates of gun-related fatalities—more than thirty-two thousand every year, according to the Brady Campaign to Prevent Gun Violence. They know that tighter controls on gun ownership will result in fewer guns on the street and fewer violent crimes committed with firearms. President Barack Obama forcefully made the case after a murderous shooting spree at a community college in Oregon in 2015:

> There is a gun for roughly every man, woman, and child in America. So how can you, with a straight face, make the argument that more guns will make us safer? We know that states with the most gun laws tend to have the fewest gun deaths. So the notion that gun laws don't work, or just will make it harder for law-abiding citizens, and criminals will still get their guns is not borne out by the evidence.[7]

Polls consistently show the people's support for gun control laws. In January 2016 a Reuters/Ipsos poll found that 63 percent of Americans said they wanted to see the next president pursue stricter gun control laws. Fifty percent approved of Obama's executive actions to tighten gun control, including steps to extend background checks on gun buyers. Six months later, following a shooting that killed forty-nine people at a gay nightclub in Orlando, Florida, poll results were even more dramatic. A poll conducted by CNN and polling firm ORC International found overall support for stricter gun laws had increased 9 percent, from 46 percent to 55 percent, in just six months. And support for specific gun control ideas was even stronger, with 92 percent in favor of expanding background checks, 87 percent approving of a ban on gun purchases by felons or those with mental health issues, and 85 percent wanting to ban sales to those on terrorist watch lists or no-fly lists.

"We know that states with the most gun laws tend to have the fewest gun deaths. So the notion that gun laws don't work, or just will make it harder for law-abiding citizens, and criminals will still get their guns is not borne out by the evidence."[7]

—President Barack Obama, following a mass shooting in Oregon in 2015

States with Stronger Gun Laws Have Fewer Gun Deaths

States with tougher gun control laws tend to rank lower in number of gun deaths. In the scatter plot, each dot represents a state. Each state is placed according to its ranking for gun control laws, from weakest laws to strongest, and its ranking in gun deaths from lowest to highest. The rankings and statistics come from the Law Center to Prevent Gun Violence.

Each state is positioned according to how it was ranked for its gun control laws, from weakest to strongest, and its 2013 gun deaths, rate rank, from lowest rate to highest.

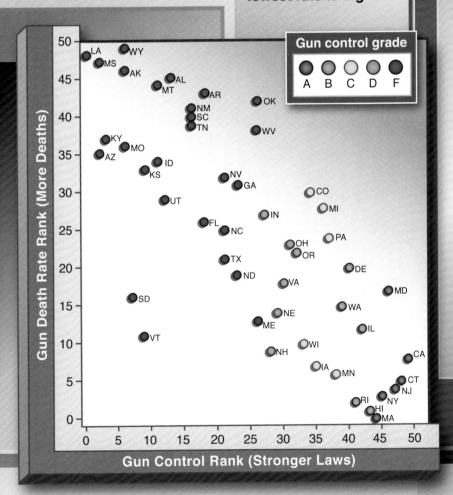

Gun control grade: A B C D F

X axis: Gun Control Rank (Stronger Laws)
Y axis: Gun Death Rate Rank (More Deaths)

Source: Slate.com, "States with Tighter Gun Control Laws Have Fewer Gun Deaths," 2015. www.slate.com.

Doubtless the murders in Orlando affected the CNN/ORC poll, but the responses also indicate that people are more than ready to see their government do something about the widespread availability of guns. After Orlando, observers pointed out that the shooter, a licensed security guard named Omar Mateen, had used a semiautomatic AR-15 rifle that he had purchased legally in Port St. Lucie, about 120 miles (193 km) from Orlando. That same weapon is banned in New York, California, and five other states. "It's a minority of states that have these type of laws in place," said Ari Freilich, an attorney at San Francisco's Law Center to Prevent Gun Violence. "The evidence is they do help."[8]

Countries with Strict Gun Control Laws

To see how effective gun control laws can be, one has only to look at countries that place tight restrictions on guns and gun ownership. According to the Geneva Declaration on Armed Violence and Development, for example, Great Britain averages between 50 and 60 gun murders a year. By contrast, in 2014 (the last year available for examination), there were 8,124 gun murders in the United States. That works out to about 160 times the British number of gun murders. Statistics rarely tell so stark a tale.

Great Britain has long taken steps to prevent gun violence. The British government regards gun ownership as a privilege, not a right. Obtaining a firearm is a rigorous, closely monitored process. Handguns are prohibited without special permission from authorities, and semiautomatic rifles are banned outright. The latter ban was enacted in 1988 following a notorious massacre in Hungerford, Berkshire—proof that national outrage over mass shootings can produce strong gun control legislation. Most firearm owners in Great Britain live in rural areas and keep shotguns for hunting or sport shooting. As a result, offenses related to firearms make up less than 0.2 percent of crimes, and British police officers famously do not carry guns themselves. Overall, Great Britain's gun control laws, which are among the world's strongest, have proved to be remarkably effective in reducing gun violence. "People say you can't unwind hundreds of years of gun history and culture [in America]," says

Andy Marsh, firearms director at Britain's Association of Chief Police Officers, "but here in the U.K., we've learned from our tragedies and taken steps to reduce the likelihood of them ever happening again."[9]

Keeping Guns out of Criminals' Hands

As Marsh suggests, changing the gun culture in America is necessary in order to remove guns from the streets. This seems like a tall task, but again a foreign country provides an example of how it might be done. Australia resembles the United States in its frontier mentality, fondness for firearms, and stress on rugged individualism. In 1996, after a decade of gun violence that saw more than one hundred victims of mass shootings in Australia, a lone gunman murdered thirty-five people and seriously wounded eighteen more at a tourist haven in Port Arthur, Tasmania. Twelve days later conservative prime minister John Howard announced a sweeping nationwide program of gun reform.

Howard convinced Australian states and territories to ban rapid-fire rifles and shotguns and pass much stricter rules for gun ownership. In addition, Howard's government used a one-time tax increase to implement a massive gun buyback, in which it collected and destroyed more than seven hundred thousand firearms across the nation. Experts estimate that fully one-third of civilian-owned guns were taken. Howard also banned imports of all new automatic and semiautomatic weapons.

> "People say you can't unwind hundreds of years of gun history and culture [in America], but here in the U.K., we've learned from our tragedies and taken steps to reduce the likelihood of them ever happening again."[9]
>
> —Andy Marsh, firearms director at Britain's Association of Chief Police Officers

Such a massive gun control effort had never been attempted before. Howard soon drew heated opposition from his conservative followers, especially in rural areas. But most Australians backed the plan. With fewer guns in the hands of criminals and ordinary citizens alike, the risk of dying from gun violence in Australia plummeted. A 2012 study by

Andrew Leigh of Australian National University and Christine Neill of Wilfrid Laurier University found that the buyback program dropped the firearm homicide rate by 59 percent and the firearm suicide rate by 65 percent. In a 2013 opinion piece for the *New York Times*, Howard said, "Today, there is a wide consensus that our 1996 reforms not only reduced the gun-related homicide rate, but also the suicide rate."[10] While he acknowledged that the situation in the United States is different from his country, he told CNN in 2015, "There's not much doubt in my mind that it's the availability of guns that causes such a high rate of murder using weapons."[11]

Reducing Suicides and Accidental Deaths

The drop in Australia's rate of suicide by firearm raises another significant point about gun control laws. Such laws can reduce not only gun murders but also suicides and accidental deaths. Many people are surprised to learn that there are nearly twice as many firearm suicides each year as firearm murders. Of the approximately thirty-two thousand gun deaths in the United States every year, about 60 percent, or more than nineteen thousand, are suicides, and 3 percent are the result of gun accidents.

According to the Law Center to Prevent Gun Violence, more than half of all suicides in the United States are committed with a firearm. In the years 2005 to 2010, an average of forty-nine gun suicides occurred each day. Experts note that about 85 percent of suicide attempts with a gun result in death. By comparison, suicide by drug overdose is fatal in less than 3 percent of cases. The combination of depression and easy availability of a gun is all too often a deadly one.

As for fatal gun accidents, they overwhelmingly occur in those under age twenty-five. Children and adolescents face even greater risk of accidental shootings due to impulsiveness, curiosity, and carelessness. An estimated 1.69 million young people age eighteen or younger live in households that contain loaded and unlocked firearms. Gun control laws that limit gun ownership, enforce gun safety rules about home storage and trigger locks, and reduce the overall number of guns in the country are desperately needed to stem the tide of needless gun fatalities.

Gun Control Laws Do Not Reduce Gun-Related Deaths

"I am not convinced that a restriction on guns of the citizens (who follow the law) will keep anyone from killing people if someone is determined to do so. Murder is 'prohibited' by the government and yet people kill. . . . Not one person has ever been saved by a 'no guns allowed' sign, and telling a criminal who wants to kill someone that he is not supposed to have a gun, will not keep him from getting a gun and killing someone."

—Jason Mosher, sheriff of Vernon County, Missouri

Jason Mosher, "Gun Laws Don't Work on People Who Break the Law," *Nevada (MO) Daily Mail*, June 18, 2016. www.nevadadailymail.com.

Consider these questions as you read:

1. How persuasive is the argument that violent crime and gun crime have fallen in the United States despite a steady increase in the number of guns? Explain.
2. Do you agree that criminals will obtain guns regardless of how strict gun control laws are? Why or why not?
3. How do you think media coverage of mass shooting incidents affects public opinion on gun control? Explain.

Editor's note: The discussion that follows presents common arguments made in support of this perspective, reinforced by facts, quotes, and examples taken from various sources.

Supporters of tighter gun control laws refuse to face facts. The main thing that gun control laws accomplish is to place more burdens and restrictions on law-abiding gun owners. As for violent gun crime, it has been going down regardless of gun laws and in spite of overall increases in gun availability. James Jacobs, director of the Center for Research in Crime and Justice at New York University School of Law, points out this basic misunderstanding about gun control in the United States:

We need to remember that we have had a remarkable decrease in violent crime and gun crime in the U.S. since the early 1990s, even though the number of firearms has increased by about 10 million every year. There's no simple correspondence between the number of firearms in private hands and the amount of gun crime, and I often find it somewhat strange that there seems to be a perception that things are worse than ever when, in reality, things are really better than they've been for decades.[12]

Mass shootings naturally bring calls for something to be done to stop them. Activists inevitably demand much stricter gun control laws, bans on assault weapons, and more extensive background checks on gun sales. But this is an emotional reaction, not a logical response. After the 2012 Newtown, Connecticut, shootings, editorial writer Ben Domenech noted:

The hard truth is that none of the proposals that politicians and commentators have made—about guns, mental health, broken homes, cultural failings, violence in mass media, and so on— could have prevented this awful crime or any other similar crime yet to take place. No law can make the murderously insane sane or remove the ability to destroy innocent life from the hands of every mentally ill American.[13]

More Guns Means Fewer Homicides

When homicide rates fall, the cause is not more gun control laws but more guns in the hands of law-abiding citizens. Between 1993 and 2013, as the number of guns per person in the United States has risen, the number of gun homicides per hundred thousand people has fallen dramatically. This decline has occurred despite wide variations in the toughness of gun laws. Gun ownership rights are more important in reducing homicides than gun control laws.

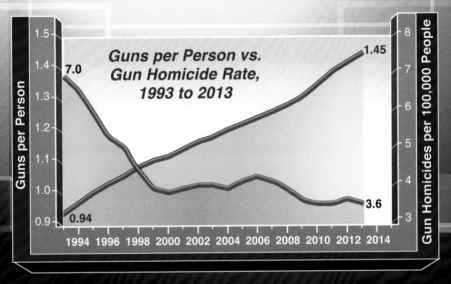

Source: American Enterprise Institute, "Chart of the Day: More Guns, Less Gun Violence Between 1993 and 2013," December 4, 2015. www.aei.org.

Pollsters observe that while a majority of Americans profess support for tougher gun laws, the approval numbers decline when the words *gun control* are used in poll questions. Americans remain leery of lawmakers trying to subvert their Second Amendment rights and to ban the sale of guns altogether.

Failure of Gun Control in Violent Cities

Gun control advocates act as if tougher gun laws are a universal cure for homicides. Yet evidence from some of America's most dangerous cities tells a different story. In 1976, for example, Washington, DC, banned the sale of handguns and ordered those who already owned firearms to keep them disassembled or trigger-locked in their homes. A police permit was required to remove trigger locks. Only police officers were authorized to carry firearms on the street. The Washington, DC, city council members hoped their sweeping ban on firearms would spread to neighboring states and eventually to the rest of the nation. Instead, their gun control effort not only failed to stop firearm violence in the city, it actually led to a rise in gun murders, from 188 in 1976 to 364 in 1988, an increase of more than 190 percent. Homicides in the city rose even further in 1993, to an appalling 454. "Washington, D.C. had some of the strictest gun laws in the country," says Florida senator Marco Rubio. "And when they passed them, violence skyrocketed."[14] Of course, the Washington, DC, handgun ban was eventually ruled unconstitutional in the Supreme Court's 2008 *District of Columbia v. Heller* decision. Today the city continues to see high rates of gun violence even though its gun control laws remain among the toughest in the nation.

Chicago, Illinois, is another large American city where strict gun laws have proved a failure. The city's grim total of 762 homicides in 2016 was the highest in the United States. In 2017 there were fourteen gun deaths in Chicago during the Fourth of July weekend, and more than one hundred people were hit by gunfire. This deadly gun violence occurred despite stringent laws about concealed carry of a handgun, background checks for gun purchasers, and selling a firearm without an owner ID card. Calls for passage of more gun laws ring hollow when evidence shows that current laws do not work.

Criminals Will Find a Way to Get Guns

As history demonstrates in cities like Washington, DC, and Chicago, gun control laws do not prevent criminals from obtaining guns. Those determined to get their hands on firearms, including criminals, gang members, and the mentally unstable, will almost always find a way. Believers in gun rights worry that gun control laws mainly inhibit law-abiding citizens from getting and using firearms to defend themselves, their families, and their homes from lawbreakers with guns. "Criminals don't obey laws," says Alan Gottlieb, founder of the group Second Amendment. "That's why we call them criminals."[15]

The fact is that criminals in cities like Chicago do not get their guns online or from gun shows, as gun control advocates contend. Instead, they obtain almost all their firearms through family members and friends. Researchers from Duke University and the University of Chicago interviewed ninety-nine inmates at Chicago's Cook County Jail who had possessed a gun illegally within six months of being incarcerated. The study found that criminals depended on people they knew and could trust when seeking firearms. "It is rare for offenders to buy from licensed dealers, and also rare for them to steal their guns," says the study. "Rather, the predominant sources of guns to offenders are family, acquaintances, fellow gang members—which is to say, members of their social network."[16] Many of these transactions are so-called straw purchases. This is when a criminal who cannot legally acquire a firearm has a friend or acquaintance with no such restriction buy the gun. Criminals also purchase guns from unlicensed street dealers who are criminals themselves.

> "It is rare for offenders to buy from licensed dealers, and also rare for them to steal their guns. Rather, the predominant sources of guns to offenders are family, acquaintances, fellow gang members—which is to say, members of their social network."[16]
>
> —A study by researchers from Duke University and the University of Chicago

High Gun Ownership Rates, Low Crime Rates

Gun control advocates often argue that the sheer number of guns in the United States represents a danger to the republic. Yet some countries also have high rates of gun ownership yet low rates of homicide. Switzerland has the fourth-most guns per capita in the world, with 2.3 million to 4.5 million firearms in a nation of more than 8 million. Despite all these guns, Switzerland has less than one gun homicide per one hundred thousand people each year. This compares with five gun homicides per one hundred thousand in the United States.

The Swiss tradition of gun ownership dates to a time when the tiny nation feared invasion and required its citizens to be armed and trained to shoot. Sales of firearms in Switzerland are regulated but mainly with safety in mind. A Swiss citizen with no criminal record and no history of mental illness can buy up to three firearms from an authorized dealer. Shooting clubs for both adults and youths are a popular pastime, and the sight of people on the street with rifles slung over their shoulders does not raise an eyebrow. The Swiss example shows that gun regulations should focus not on banning weapons, but on promoting the safe and responsible use of rifles and handguns.

Chapter Two

Should Background Checks for Gun Buyers Be Expanded?

Background Checks for Gun Buyers Should Be Expanded

- Universal background checks will help curb gun sales by unlicensed private sellers.
- Data shows that expanding background checks reduces mass shootings and gun violence.
- Law-abiding gun owners have nothing to fear from slightly more extensive background checks.

The Debate at a Glance

Background Checks for Gun Buyers Should Not Be Expanded

- Federally licensed gun sellers already are required to do extensive background checks on gun buyers.
- Extending the three-day waiting period for buying a gun is an unfair restriction on a law-abiding citizen's right to own a gun.
- The American Civil Liberties Union (ACLU) is concerned that government background checks could lead to a national gun registry and surveillance on legal gun owners.

Background Checks for Gun Buyers Should Be Expanded

"By far the most dangerous gap in federal firearms laws today is the background check loophole. Although federal law requires licensed firearms dealers to perform background checks on prospective purchasers, it does not require unlicensed sellers to do so. An estimated 40% of all firearms transferred in the US are acquired from unlicensed sellers without a background check."

—The Law Center to Prevent Gun Violence

The Law Center to Prevent Gun Violence, "Universal Background Checks," 2017. http://smartgunlaws.org.

Consider these questions as you read:

1. What criteria should be used to determine if laws about background checks are effective? Which is most important?
2. Do you believe that an expanded system of background checks could prevent criminals from getting guns? Why or why not?
3. Does a waiting period for legally buying a gun violate a citizen's Second Amendment rights? Explain.

Editor's note: The discussion that follows presents common arguments made in support of this perspective, reinforced by facts, quotes, and examples taken from various sources.

Of all gun control measures, expanding background checks for gun buyers does the best in opinion polls. In a 2015 Gallup poll, 86 percent of respondents favored universal background checks for all gun purchases in the United States. Other polls show more than 90 percent support. This compares to much narrower margins for measures such as banning assault weapons or high-capacity bullet magazines. The public's overwhelming support for more extensive background checks would seem to make passing a new law in Congress an easy matter, particularly after a series of high-profile mass shootings. Yet a majority of representatives in Congress still resist expanding the current system. They claim that a reasonable pursuit of criminal gun purchasers would mainly tend to harass legal buyers from exercising their rights under the Second Amendment. But background checks do not prevent the lawful purchase of firearms; they instead create a system in which such purchases can proceed in an orderly fashion with reasonable government oversight.

> "As a firm believer of the 2nd Amendment, I support the reasonable expansion of National Instant Criminal Background System (NICS) checks into secondary and private markets for the purpose of keeping firearms out of the wrong hands."[17]
>
> —Former US senator Tom Coburn in a 2013 letter to Senate colleagues

Even many pro-gun conservatives understand that for the background check system to work, it must be expanded to include all sellers of firearms, including unlicensed dealers online and at gun shows and flea markets. In a 2013 letter to his Senate colleagues, now-retired Republican senator Tom Coburn put it this way:

> As a firm believer of the 2nd Amendment, I support the reasonable expansion of National Instant Criminal Background System (NICS) checks into secondary and private markets for the purpose of keeping firearms out of the wrong hands. . . . The more than $1 billion in federal tax dollars spent on creating and maintaining the National Instant Criminal Background Check System is rendered useless when a prohibited purchaser can just as easily procure a firearm from a gun show or an internet marketplace without a NICS check as they can at gun stores.[17]

Under the current system, the federal agency that licenses gun dealers is the Bureau of Alcohol, Tobacco, Firearms and Explosives. All gun

Mandatory Background Checks Save Lives

States that require comprehensive background checks for gun buyers have far fewer instances of fatal gun violence than states without comprehensive background checks. Nineteen states plus the District of Columbia mandate a background check for every handgun sale. Statistics show that background checks save lives by reducing gun violence, which is why such practices should be expanded nationwide.

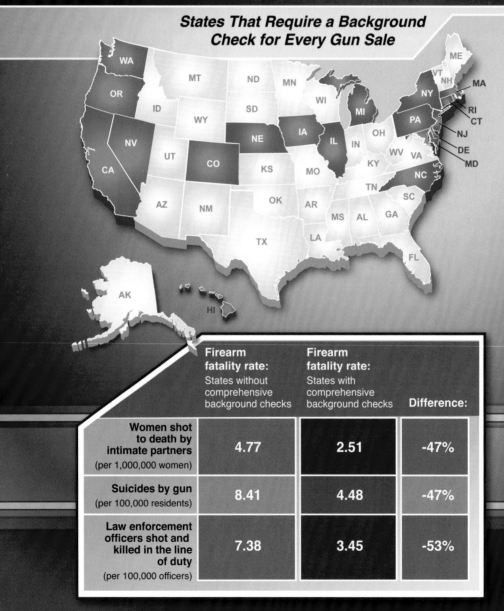

States That Require a Background Check for Every Gun Sale

	Firearm fatality rate: States without comprehensive background checks	Firearm fatality rate: States with comprehensive background checks	Difference:
Women shot to death by intimate partners (per 1,000,000 women)	4.77	2.51	-47%
Suicides by gun (per 100,000 residents)	8.41	4.48	-47%
Law enforcement officers shot and killed in the line of duty (per 100,000 officers)	7.38	3.45	-53%

Source: Everytown for Gun Safety, "Background Checks Reduce Gun Violence and Save Lives," January 1, 2017. https://everytownresearch.org.

dealers are required to have a license, whether they market guns online, in stores, or at gun shows. Gun dealers must also perform background checks on prospective firearm buyers, maintain records of all firearm sales, make records available for inspection by law enforcement, and report the loss or theft of a weapon from the license holder's stock.

Unlicensed and informal gun sellers, however, are required to do none of these things. These sales often fall through the cracks. Illegal sales also occur due to a federal law that requires government researchers to complete background checks within three business days. If the check takes longer, a gun dealer can go ahead and complete the sale even to a questionable buyer. Between 1999 and 2012 about thirty-six hundred guns a year nationwide were sold to individuals who ultimately failed a delayed background check. Such problems could be almost eliminated with a more extensive and efficient system.

Curbing Gun Sales by Unlicensed Private Sellers

The main purpose of expanding background checks is to address the problem of unlicensed private sellers. The original Gun Control Act of 1968 required licenses for persons "engaged in the business" of selling firearms. However, the law set up loopholes for those who make "occasional sales, exchanges, or purchases of firearms for the enhancement of a personal collection or for a hobby."[18] Today this loophole has become a wide superhighway for unlicensed dealers who claim to be hobbyists while trafficking all sorts of guns to criminals, terrorists, and the mentally ill.

Experts estimate that these unlicensed, so-called private sellers, with no obligation to perform background checks on potential buyers, account for 40 percent of firearms sold in the United States. Of course, the merchandising of guns on the Internet has made it much easier for criminals to locate sellers willing to transfer guns to them with no background check. According to Third Way, a public policy think tank, unlicensed private sellers list more than sixty-seven thousand guns for sale online. Nearly one-third of the ads on Armslist, a website for gun sales, are posted by private sellers who sell in high volume and post numerous ads over a two-month period. Investigations indicate that private online sellers often agree to sell even when the buyer admits to problems in passing a background check.

Lax standards regarding background checks can have tragic consequences. In 2013, Radcliffe Haughton was able to buy a $500 handgun from a private seller he found online despite being ineligible to do so because of a restraining order against him for domestic violence. Haughton later took the weapon to the spa where his wife, Zina, worked. There he shot and killed Zina and two of her coworkers and wounded four other women before killing himself. Haughton is just the sort of dangerously unstable person that the universal background check system is designed to foil. Shortly after the murders, Zina's brother, Elvin Daniel, himself a member of the NRA, said, "I feel that had there been a background check, had that been in place, my sister would still be with us today."[19]

> "I feel that had there been a background check, had that been in place, my sister would still be with us today."[19]
>
> —Elvin Daniel, brother of Zina Haughton, who was shot and killed by her abusive husband

Universal Background Checks Work

The bottom line is that background checks are very effective in reducing homicides and gun violence. Expanding the system and closing loopholes will only improve these results. Data from several centers that track gun violence, including the Centers for Disease Control and Prevention, makes the point emphatically. For the years 1999 to 2014, the fifteen states with background check laws had a fatality rate from firearms of 7.98 per 100,000. This compares with a rate of 12.23 per 100,000 for the other thirty-five states, a difference of about 35 percent. States with universal background check laws also have 38 percent fewer homicides of women shot by intimate partners and 53 percent fewer suicides by firearm.

Further evidence comes from the states of Missouri and Connecticut. In 2007 Missouri repealed a long-standing law that made background checks mandatory for all purchases of firearms. Researchers at

Johns Hopkins University found that the repeal brought grim results: a 23 percent rise in gun deaths, which works out to between fifty-five and sixty-three additional gun deaths each year. Significantly, there was no increase in homicides unrelated to guns. In 2015 the pro–gun control group Everytown for Gun Safety also found that since the law's repeal, more guns used in crimes in Missouri were purchased inside the state. Meanwhile, a separate study showed that when Connecticut passed a background check law much like the one Missouri abandoned, gun homicides in Connecticut plummeted by 40 percent. "All of these signals are telling you that guns sold in the state of Missouri are more readily available for criminal misuse," says Daniel Webster, who participated in studies of both states' gun laws. "You had a system that wasn't perfect, but it was blocking a lot of risky transactions, and then you said, 'OK, no more accountability.'"[20]

Lawful Gun Owners Have Nothing to Fear

The pro–gun rights lobby ignores the effectiveness of background check laws. Members of this lobby resort to misleading arguments about how expanding background checks and enforcing waiting periods for gun purchases will trample on people's Second Amendment rights. But the truth is that law-abiding gun owners have nothing to fear from strong laws on background checks. And, as polls show, most responsible gun owners know it.

Such gun owners understand the importance of keeping firearms out of the wrong hands. Undergoing a background check and three-day waiting period is a small price to pay to prevent mass shootings and other gun violence. Claims that expanding background checks will lead to firearm bans or confiscation of guns are just hysterical propaganda. Instead, the system will extend the same set of rules to all gun buyers. As President Barack Obama said in 2016:

> If a father wants to teach his daughter how to hunt, he can walk into a gun store, get a background check, purchase his weapon safely and responsibly. . . . The problem is some gun sellers have

been operating under a different set of rules. A violent felon can buy the exact same weapon over the Internet with no background check, no questions asked. . . . So we've created a system in which dangerous people are allowed to play by a different set of rules than a responsible gun owner who buys his or her gun the right way and subjects themselves to a background check. That doesn't make sense. Everybody should have to abide by the same rules.[21]

Background Checks for Gun Buyers Should Not Be Expanded

"Background checks, like all gun-control laws, focus on the law-abiding while mostly ignoring criminals. The idea that it makes sense to expand these wasteful and ineffective money sponges to include private transactions between law-abiding citizens is ridiculous and an affront to liberty."

—Jeff Knox, director of the Firearms Coalition

Jeff Knox, "Why Background Checks Don't Work," World Net Daily, March 5, 2015. www.wnd.com.

Consider these questions as you read:

1. What is your view of the argument that expanding background checks would hinder law-abiding gun buyers while doing nothing to stop criminals from getting guns?
2. How can the government prevent private transfer of firearms to convicted felons or the mentally ill? Should friends or family members be prosecuted for such transfers?
3. Do you believe that a national database for gun owners is an invasion of privacy? Why or why not?

Editor's note: The discussion that follows presents common arguments made in support of this perspective, reinforced by facts, quotes, and examples taken from various sources.

A system of background checks for gun purchasers is a good idea in theory, but it is only partly effective in practice. Gun control advocates constantly push for expanding the system in order to reach private sellers and collectors, but such an expansion would result in all sorts of new problems. James Jacobs, director of the Center for Research in Crime and Justice at

Enforcement of Existing Gun Laws Is All That Is Needed

New gun control laws, including expanded background checks, are not needed. What is needed is for states to enforce the laws already on the books. In 2013, law enforcement agencies in Pennsylvania began to crack down on prospective gun buyers who lied on background checks. The next year, investigations of these people soared to more than four thousand, and the number of arrests doubled. For the previous decade, investigations and arrests had averaged much less than one thousand per year. Other states should follow Pennsylvania's example and enforce existing laws rather than adding new ones.

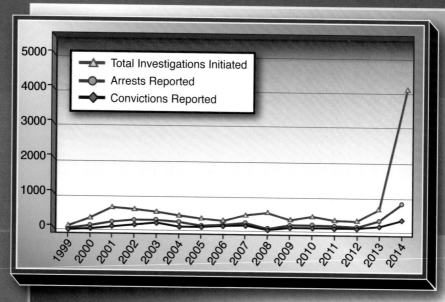

Source: The Trace, "Banned from Owning Guns, Many 'Lie and Try' to Buy Them Anyway. Few Are Punished for the Crime," May 9, 2016. www.thetrace.org.

New York University and a professor of constitutional law, notes that no simple policy change will magically reduce gun crimes. There are always too many problems in implementing new laws and enforcing them.

Studies on the effects of background checks are generally inconclusive. Gun control advocates point to studies of laws in Missouri and Connecticut that seem to establish the effectiveness of background checks. Yet these studies do not focus on background checks alone. They actually deal with permits to purchase firearms, in which gun buyers first have to obtain a permit from local law enforcement, a process that includes getting a background check. Having to go through local police is probably more of a deterrent to illegal buyers than getting checked at a typical gun store.

The NRA's Wayne LaPierre and other supporters of gun rights argue that the United States has enough gun laws already. Instead of expanding background checks—and introducing new curbs on lawful gun buyers—they suggest enforcing the laws already on the books. For example, the federal government rarely prosecutes attempted gun purchasers who are rejected after background checks. Giving false information in an attempt to buy a firearm is a felony. Statistics show that rejected gun buyers are far more likely to commit a violent crime after being denied. Nonetheless, according to the US Department of Justice, in 2010 only forty-four individuals out of more than eighty thousand denials were recommended for prosecution. It is hard to take background checks seriously when rejected buyers—those who *lie and try*, according to law enforcement officials—can simply redirect their efforts to obtain guns elsewhere. "This is not like looking for a needle in a haystack," says John Feinblatt, an official with the group Mayors Against Illegal Guns. "Once they have been rejected, they go online or to a private seller or gun show and get a gun."[22]

Would Not Have Stopped Mass Shooters

Gun control activists insist that mass shootings continue to occur because Congress refuses to pass universal background checks for gun buyers. These activists seem to believe that an expanded system would keep guns out of the hands of dangerous individuals. However, according to experts who have studied the issue closely, expanding background checks actually would make no difference.

Universal background checks are aimed at stopping the private transfer of guns outside the regulated system—the so-called "gun show loophole." Yet a 2016 study by the Crime Prevention Research Center questions the effectiveness of a universal system. "Despite the frequent calls for expanded background checks after mass public shootings, there is no evidence that background checks on private transfers of guns would have prevented any of the attacks that have taken place since at least

> "Despite the frequent calls for expanded background checks after mass public shootings, there is no evidence that background checks on private transfers of guns would have prevented any of the attacks that have taken place since at least 2000."[23]
>
> —A 2016 study by the Crime Prevention Research Center

2000,"[23] the study declares. The authors of the study also found no statistical evidence that such mass shootings happen less frequently in states with background checks on private gun transfers.

The problem is that mass shooters almost always use firearms that were purchased from licensed dealers by lawful buyers who were cleared by background checks. For example, Adam Lanza, the gunman in the 2012 Newtown grade school shootings, used firearms that his mother had purchased legally with a background check. The couple who killed fourteen people in 2015 in San Bernardino, California, obtained guns from a friend who also passed a background check. That friend was later charged with lying about his plans to transfer the weapons, but no background check would have uncovered any irregularity. Chris Harper-Mercer, who shot and killed nine people at an Oregon community college in 2015, employed guns that he and certain relatives purchased after passing the federal background checks.

In the few cases when a shooter should have been prevented from buying a gun, the sales went through not because of loopholes in background checks but because of simple administrative errors. Dylann Roof, who murdered nine people in a South Carolina church in 2015, should have been flagged for a prior drug possession arrest, but his gun purchase went through when a federal examiner did not notice the arrest report. Such incidents show that rather than passing new gun laws that burden law-abiding owners, the laws already on the books should be properly enforced.

Waiting Periods Are an Unfair Restriction

Another change to background check procedures that gun control advocates seek is setting up a mandatory waiting period and extending it up to ten days. The purpose of the waiting period is twofold. First, it provides time for the FBI to complete a background check of the prospective buyer. Second, and more controversially, it supposedly creates a "'cooling off' period to help guard against impulsive acts of violence—especially suicide,"[24] according to the Law Center to Prevent Gun Violence. However, a mandatory waiting period mainly furthers the anti–gun lobby's goal of making it more difficult for law-abiding citizens to purchase firearms.

Currently, under the National Instant Criminal Background Check System, there is no required waiting period. Once a background check is complete—and many are done in minutes—a buyer is free to take home his or her newly purchased firearm. Sometimes a background check takes longer. In such cases the FBI has three business days to complete the check before the gun must be delivered to the buyer. Critics complain that this results in certain gun purchasers receiving firearms without a completed background check. They suggest a mandatory ten-day waiting period, as in California state law, or even a period of one month. But such changes would place unfair restrictions on lawful gun buyers who seek guns for self-defense or home protection. Beth Baumann, who works for a concealed-carry holsters company, notes that extended waiting periods are especially misguided with regard to longtime gun owners. "It doesn't matter if they already own and operate a firearm or if they have a concealed carry weapon permit," she says. "They are treated as though they have never purchased a firearm before."[25]

> "It doesn't matter if [longtime gun owners] already own and operate a firearm or if they have a concealed carry weapon permit. They are treated as though they have never purchased a firearm before."[25]
>
> —Beth Baumann, representative for a concealed-carry holsters company

Privacy Issues with Background Checks

Expanding background checks also would raise privacy issues for legal gun buyers. Those in favor of expansion want detailed records kept of gun sales nationwide. Gun owners fear this could lead to a national gun registry, as a first step to a program for confiscating firearms. But civil libertarians also worry that firearm ownership records and background checks could lead to government surveillance of gun owners and potential problems with invasion of privacy.

Anonymity is crucial to gun owners. They want to be safe from criminals seeking to steal their guns and free from neighborhood gossip about their choice to keep firearms. Records of a background check rejection due to past treatment for mental illness could also be abused. According to Chris Calabrese, a lobbyist for the ACLU, "You just worry that you're going to see searches of the databases and an expansion for purposes that were not intended when the information was collected."[26] The ACLU also has expressed concern that gun transfers could be interpreted too broadly under an expanded system. Legal gun owners might inadvertently break the law when lending a gun to a friend on a hunting trip or at a shooting range. Implementing universal background checks is likely to infringe the rights of law-abiding citizens who choose to own guns.

Chapter Three

Should Military-Style Assault Weapons Be Banned?

Military-Style Assault Weapons Should Not Be Banned

- Fully automatic assault rifles are already banned in the United States. Semiautomatic rifles shoot once with each pull of the trigger, like any other gun.
- Banning high-capacity magazines for so-called assault weapons is futile, since so many already exist.
- As the number of so-called assault weapons and large magazines has increased, firearm-related crime has actually fallen.

The Debate at a Glance

Military-Style Assault Weapons Should Be Banned

- Assault weapons are designed for lethal power and accuracy in military operations and are not necessary for home protection or sport shooting.
- Most mass shootings involve assault weapons with large-capacity magazines, enabling the shooter to keep firing without reloading.
- Lax US laws lead to smuggling of assault weapons to Latin America and other areas.

Military-Style Assault Weapons Should Not Be Banned

"After the [expiration of the 1994] assault weapons ban, guns were supposed to flood the streets and just start killing people. Crime was supposed to skyrocket. But that's not what happened. Yes, Americans bought a ton of rifles after the law expired, but rather than going up, the number of homicides in which rifles were used drastically fell. There were way more guns, but way less crime."

—Sean Davis, editor and cofounder of the *Federalist* online magazine

Sean Davis, "The Assault Weapons Ban Is a Stupid Idea Pushed by Stupid People," *Federalist*, June 13, 2016. http://smartgunlaws.org.

Consider these questions as you read:

1. Do you agree that calls to ban assault weapons after mass shootings are mostly emotional arguments? Why or why not?
2. How persuasive is the argument that assault weapons for sale today are not machine guns and therefore should remain legal? Explain.
3. Do you believe firearms fitted with high-capacity magazines are suitable for ordinary gun owners? Why or why not?

Editor's note: The discussion that follows presents common arguments made in support of this perspective, reinforced by facts, quotes, and examples taken from various sources.

One of the most misleading debates related to gun control involves so-called military-style assault weapons. The anti–gun lobby has exploited the optics of what many non-gun owners consider to be scary-looking guns. These are rifles equipped with features such as adjustable stocks, pistol grips, and larger bullet magazines, making them appear like the kind of weapons used by modern soldiers on the battlefield. When a gun of this type is used in a mass shooting, the inevitable calls to ban these so-called assault weapons ring out on social media and in the national press. To hear the critics, it is as if the rifle made its own way into a crowded school or nightclub and opened fire with no warning. Or rather, they make it sound as though the NRA was pulling the trigger.

"Prayers are not enough," tweeted actress Susan Sarandon following the June 12, 2016, shooting at a gay nightclub in Orlando, Florida. "Time for a ban on automatic weapons. There is only one reason they exist and that is to kill our fellow man."[27] In reality, however, the main weapon used in Orlando—a standard AR-15 rifle, one of the best-selling guns in the United States—was not automatic but semiautomatic. And such rifles are favored by hunters and recreational shooters, as well as by those seeking to protect themselves, their loved ones, and their property. "A lot of the media calls them assault rifles," says Brian Ludlow, owner of the Indy Trading Post, a store licensed to sell guns. "Assault is an action, it's not a description. So the NRA, myself, and everyone here chooses to call them modern sporting rifles."[28]

> "A lot of the media calls them assault rifles. Assault is an action, it's not a description. So the NRA, myself, and everyone here chooses to call them modern sporting rifles."[28]
>
> —Brian Ludlow, owner of the Indy Trading Post, a store licensed to sell guns

The mass shooting in Orlando was caused not by a certain type of weapon but by a person inflamed with a hateful ideology. Omar Mateen, who murdered forty-nine people and wounded fifty-three others in the nightclub, had pledged allegiance to ISIS, the radical Islamist group. Radicals, racists, and the mentally ill have committed mass murder using everything from guns, knives, and bombs to large vehicles. Should we next consider banning panel trucks for their potential use as a deadly weapon?

Automatic Rifles Already Banned

Gun control advocates seem to believe that military-style machine guns are commonly found in the United States and are widely available to criminals

Support for Banning Assault Weapons at Record Low

Gun ownership is a constitutional right—and Americans are growing tired of laws that violate that right. This can be seen in polls measuring support for assault weapons. The number of Americans in favor of banning the manufacture, sale, or possession of semiautomatic rifles, or assault rifles, is at an all-time low. The number of Americans in favor of such a ban fell from 44 percent in 2012 to 36 percent in 2016.

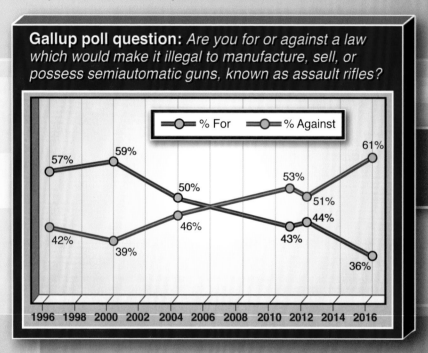

Gallup poll question: *Are you for or against a law which would make it illegal to manufacture, sell, or possess semiautomatic guns, known as assault rifles?*

Source: Gallup, "In U.S., Support for Assault Weapons Ban at Record Low," October 26, 2016. www.gallup.com.

and terrorists. In the aftermath of the Orlando massacre, Florida representative Alan Grayson claimed in an interview on CNN that the AR-15 rifle used in the shooting was able to fire 700 rounds per minute, an assertion also made by the BBC. Firearm experts were quick to correct this absurd exaggeration. The semiautomatic AR-15 fires only 1 round with each squeeze of the trigger; it does not fire continuously like a machine gun. To fire 700 rounds in a minute, the gunman would have had to go through 23 bullet-holding magazines of 30 rounds each, an average of 11.53 rounds per second. "Not to mention, you'd have to sustain this for a full 60 seconds, no time factored for changing magazines," wrote one reader of the conservative website American Crossroads. "Wow. That's impressive."[29]

Moreover, sales of fully automatic guns—those that continue to fire as long as the user holds down the trigger—already are banned everywhere in the United States. In fact, machine guns have been strictly regulated in America since passage of the National Firearms Act of 1934, in the days of violent gangsters like Al Capone and Pretty Boy Floyd. Weapons of today that operate like a machine gun include the US military's M16 rifle, which can be adjusted to automatic or semiautomatic mode. The M16 is a sophisticated, high-powered weapon with a hefty price tag to match. It is not available at the local Walmart. By contrast, the widely owned semiautomatic AR-15, which bears a superficial resemblance to the M16, is not high powered. It uses the same caliber of ammunition as many other sporting guns. When gun control advocates rail about military-style guns proliferating on American streets, they generally do not know what they are talking about.

Banning High-Capacity Magazines Is Futile

The push to eliminate assault weapons also extends to a proposed ban on high-capacity magazines that hold more than ten rounds. But like so many ill-considered gun control schemes, such a ban would be futile. According to the NRA's Institute for Legislative Action:

> Americans already own tens of millions of magazines that hold more than 10 rounds. If the manufacture of new such magazines were banned, the cost of pre-ban magazines would rise (as it did when the 1994 ban was imposed), but any criminal determined to have them would always be able to get them, including by theft from law-abiding owners. A criminal could carry multiple limited-capacity magazines and use them to reload a firearm quickly.[30]

So ridding the country of high-capacity magazines would require some sort of federal confiscation effort—the sort of action that occurs mainly in authoritarian regimes. Such a ban could also have unintended consequences. As the NRA points out, the 1994 federal law that set the ten-round limit for magazines led many gun owners to switch to more powerful handguns. Instead of holding from thirteen to seventeen rounds of small-caliber bullets, magazines for these handguns could instead hold ten rounds of large-caliber ammunition, making the weapon more lethal. This change became widely adopted. Also, it is a matter of little skill for a criminal to fashion a higher-capacity magazine for personal use.

> "Realize that you will never shoot as well as your score at the range when you are under the unbelievable stress of a life-or-death encounter. Which would you prefer to have in your magazine in such an event? Ten rounds? Or fifteen or seventeen? Or perhaps even 30?"[31]
>
> —Rabbi Dovid Bendory of Jews for the Preservation of Firearms Ownership

Finally, the individual gun owner should have the right to keep firearms with high-capacity magazines for self-defense. Most of the time such a magazine is not needed, but in a crisis it may be essential. For example, a gun owner may be faced with multiple assailants in a home invasion or a street confrontation. "Realize that you will never shoot as well as your score at the range when you are under the unbelievable stress of a life-or-death encounter," notes Rabbi Dovid Bendory of Jews for the Preservation of Firearms Ownership. "Which would you prefer to have in your magazine in such an event? Ten rounds? Or fifteen or seventeen? Or perhaps even 30?"[31]

More Assault Weapons, Less Crime

One of the strongest arguments against a ban on so-called assault weapons is based on statistics comparing gun ownership and crime rates. From 1991 to 2013 the number of AR-15 semiautomatic rifles in the United States—the firearm that gun control advocates demonize as the chief assault weapon—rose by more than 4.5 million. Semiautomatic firearms of all kinds rose by more than 50 million. The total number of firearms in private hands rose by more than 130 million. Yet during that period, total violent crime decreased by 49 percent to a forty-year low. According to economist Mark Perry of the American Enterprise Institute, gun homicide rates also declined by 49 percent, from 7 to 3.6 per 100,000 people. Despite a populace that owns more guns than ever before—and that includes semiautomatic rifles—gun crimes in America have plummeted overall.

Homicides committed by so-called assault rifles showed similar declines. From 2010 to 2014 sales of the AR-15 increased 28 percent per year, as the *Los Angeles Times* recently reported. Yet the numbers for confirmed deaths by rifle fell from 367 in 2010 to only 248 in 2014. "The data produce one inescapable conclusion," writes Andrew Cline, a reporter for the *Federalist*. "The entire premise for a new 'assault weapons' ban—that the proliferation of 'assault weapons' has led to unprecedented carnage—is completely untrue."[32]

Military-Style Assault Weapons Should Be Banned

"When the framers wrote of 'arms,' they . . . could not have foreseen modern rifles or high-capacity magazines. . . . No hunter needs an AR-15 to bring down a deer. None of us needs such a weapon to defend our families against intruders."

—Eugene Robinson, editorial writer for the *Washington Post*, following the mass shooting in Orlando, Florida

Eugene Robinson, "Assault Weapons Must Be Banned in America," *Washington Post*, June 13, 2016. www.washingtonpost.com.

Consider these questions as you read:

1. Why do you think gun control advocates have failed to convince Congress to reinstitute the 1994 ban on assault weapons?
2. Do you believe that a ban on assault weapons would lead to a similar ban on other large guns such as hunting rifles? Why or why not?
3. Should victims of shooters armed with an assault rifle and a high-capacity magazine be able to sue the manufacturer of the gun? Why or why not?

Editor's note: The discussion that follows presents common arguments made in support of this perspective, reinforced by facts, quotes, and examples taken from various sources.

Mass shootings occur now in America with sickening frequency. And they are all too often perpetrated with an assault weapon. The magazine *Mother Jones* found that assault weapons were used in seven of the last eight high-profile mass shootings in the United States. The usual culprit is the AR-15—the Orlando killer employed an especially lethal Sig Sauer version of this gun. A military-grade combat rifle like the AR-15 has no place in a civilized society. Joshua Koskoff, a lawyer who is suing the rifle's manufacturer on behalf of families who lost loved ones in the Sandy Hook Elementary School shooting in 2012, emphasizes how deadly the AR-15 can be. "It is the gold standard for killing the enemy in battle," says Koskoff, "just as it has become the gold standard for mass murder of innocent civilians."[33] Nonetheless, virtually anyone of legal age can buy this rifle at thousands of outlets throughout the United States.

It was not always so. In 1994 President Bill Clinton signed into law the Public Safety and Recreational Firearms Use Protection Act, which banned the sale of military-style assault weapons and large-capacity magazines. Democrats paid a high political price for the ban, and in 2004 a Republican-led Congress allowed the law to expire. Yet multiple studies have shown that the federal ban was a success, especially with regard to keeping assault weapons out of criminal hands. According to the Law Center to Prevent Gun Violence, several major cities saw the number of assault weapons among recovered guns used in crimes fall by at least 32 percent after the federal ban took effect. John A. Tures, a political science professor at LaGrange College in Georgia, also found evidence of the law's positive effect. In the years 2005 to 2015, after the ban expired, there were 46 mass shootings, an average of 4.18 per year. This compares to an average of only 1.6 mass shootings per year during the ban.

Although the gun control lobby has repeatedly pushed for a new, more comprehensive ban on assault weapons, legislators' fears about backlash from gun owners and the NRA have so far stalled the effort. Those committed to gun control must do a better job of explaining to the public how bans on assault weapons have worked in other places, including Europe and Australia. In the interest of public safety, these terrible weapons must be removed from American streets once and for all.

Designed for Lethal Power and Accuracy

NRA spokespeople and other gun rights advocates often dispute the characterization of guns like the AR-15 as assault weapons. They claim that gun control activists are merely overreacting to what looks like a scary gun. But the features that make the AR-15 an effective assault weapon are there to enhance the killing potential of the shooter. They are also mostly unnecessary for hunting or sport shooting.

For example, the gun industry contends that the AR-15 is not like a military weapon because it cannot be fired continuously with a single press of the trigger. Yet industry people know this rifle is actually more deadly in its semiautomatic mode. Munitions experts refer to the AR-15's semiautomatic capability as *one-shot, one-kill* due to its lethal power and accuracy. Reporter Sarah Zhang, who researched the physics of AR-15 gunfire with trauma surgeons who have seen the results, says:

> The bullet from a handgun is—absurd as it may sound—slow compared to that from an AR-15. . . . The bullet from an AR-15 does an entirely different kind of violence to the human body. It's relatively small, but it leaves the muzzle at three times the speed of a handgun bullet. It has so much energy that it can disintegrate three inches of leg bone. . . . And the exit wound can be a nasty, jagged hole the size of an orange.[34]

> **"The bullet from a handgun is—absurd as it may sound—slow compared to that from an AR-15. . . . The bullet from an AR-15 does an entirely different kind of violence to the human body."[34]**
>
> —Sarah Zhang, reporter for *Wired* online magazine

The AR-15 also allows the shooter to fire many bullets one by one very rapidly while still maintaining control of the weapon. Its pistol grip enables the shooter to fire from the shoulder or the hip. The rifle is designed with a barrel shroud—a covering that partially or fully encircles the gun barrel—that allows the shooter to steady the weapon with the non-trigger hand without getting burns from a hot barrel. It can also be fitted with a high-capacity magazine to extend the number of available rounds before needing to be reloaded. Bernie Horn, senior adviser at the Public Leadership Institute, writes:

> The parts or features of an assault weapon are not there to look scary (as the NRA suggests); they are there to make it possible for

the shooter to do scary things. With these features, any deranged person can empty a 30-round magazine as fast as he or she can pull the trigger while maintaining control of the gun—and then quickly insert another fully-loaded magazine. Which is exactly what happened in Orlando.[35]

Large-Capacity Magazines Are Not Necessary

The arguments for high-capacity magazines made by gun rights advocates border on the absurd. Plainly, no gun owner needs so many rounds in one magazine. The NRA touts the AR-15 as a hunting rifle, but hunters fire at most one or two rounds at a deer before it falls or flees. In fact, traditional hunting rifles have a bolt-action or lever-action feature that calls for the shooter to manually load each round. Large clips of bullets add nothing to a hunter's sport.

The other frequent claim is that large-capacity magazines are necessary for self-defense. Fears that housebreaking criminals might be armed with thirty-round magazines supposedly require gun owners, in the interest of personal safety, to have the same capability. However, this arms race theory of home protection lacks logic. The idea of a homeowner losing a shootout with an intruder or even a gang of intruders because he or she had to stop to reload sounds more like a Hollywood movie than a genuine concern. It does not compare to the all-too-real danger of a deranged shooter firing away at innocent people using an AR-15 fitted with a high-capacity clip. Some magazines hold as many as one hundred rounds, thus posing an even greater threat. As the Law Center to Prevent Gun Violence notes, "The

> "The parts or features of an assault weapon are not there to look scary (as the NRA suggests); they are there to make it possible for the shooter to do scary things. With these features, any deranged person can empty a 30-round magazine as fast as he or she can pull the trigger while maintaining control of the gun."[35]
>
> —Bernie Horn, senior adviser at the Public Leadership Institute

Mass Shooting Deaths are Rising Since Expiration of Assault Weapons Ban

Since the US ban on assault weapons expired in 2004, the number of fatalities from mass shootings and the frequency of the deadliest mass shootings have increased. Banning the manufacture, sale, and possession of assault weapons helped limit the number of mass shootings overall. This ban must be reinstated.

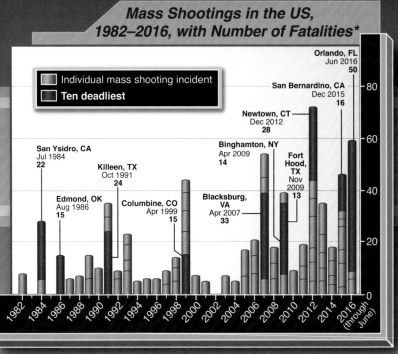

Mass Shootings in the US, 1982–2016, with Number of Fatalities*

*Shootings with three or more fatalities. Prior to January 2013, shootings with four or more fatalities.

Source: *The Economist*, "Counting America's Mass Shootings," June 13, 2016. www.economist.com.

time required to reload can be critical in enabling victims to escape and law enforcement or others to intervene."[36]

Smuggling Assault Weapons Across the US Border

The NRA continues to downplay the importance of military-style features on assault weapons. But the NRA is not the only group that approves of America's lax policy toward assault weapons. Mexico's drug cartels receive a huge benefit in the form of smuggled assault rifles and semiautomatic handguns pouring across the border. A 2016 report from the Government Accountability Office announced that 70 percent of all crime-related guns recovered in Mexico from 2009 to 2014 could be traced back to the United States. This represented a total of more than seventy thousand guns, many of them the high-caliber assault rifles drug traffickers prefer. Since the Mexican government does not attempt to trace every recovered firearm through the Bureau of Alcohol, Tobacco, Firearms and Explosives, the actual total is probably even higher.

As far back as 2010, Mexican president Felipe Calderón made a speech to the US Congress in which he urged lawmakers to restore the federal ban on assault weapons. Later he told CNN, "The criminals have become more and more vicious in their eagerness to spark fear and anxiety in society. One of the main factors that allows criminals to strengthen themselves is the unlimited access to high-powered weapons, which are sold freely, and also indiscriminately, in the United States of America."[37] Not only does the widespread availability of assault weapons in the United States lead to mass shootings and other violence, it also threatens innocent lives in Mexico and other Latin American countries where drug lords terrorize the people. These awful weapons must be banned at once.

Chapter Four

Should Individuals Have the Right to Carry a Concealed Handgun?

Individuals Should Have the Right to Carry a Concealed Handgun

- Criminals are less likely to attack a person whom they believe may be armed.
- Most adults who legally carry a concealed handgun are law-abiding and responsible gun owners.
- Concealed carry is important in promoting safety for women.

The Debate at a Glance

Individuals Should Not Have the Right to Carry a Concealed Handgun

- Concealed carry leads to more gun crimes and deaths from gun accidents.
- Concealed handguns increase the likelihood that arguments and disputes will become deadly.
- Stopping crime is the job of law enforcement, not the individual handgun owner.

Individuals Should Have the Right to Carry a Concealed Handgun

"It isn't any coincidence that crime rates started to go down when concealed carry was permitted. Just the idea that criminals don't know who is armed and who isn't has a deterrent effect."

—Richard Pearson, executive director of the Illinois State Rifle Association

Quoted in *Investor's Business Daily*, "Chicago Crime Rate Drops, Thanks to Concealed Carry," September 2, 2014. www.investors.com.

Consider these questions as you read:

1. Why do you think a majority of Americans support the individual right to carry a concealed weapon, and what is your view of this issue?
2. Do you believe that the Second Amendment gives Americans the right to carry a loaded handgun in public? Why or why not?
3. Taking into account the facts and ideas in this discussion, are you persuaded that concealed carry helps reduce crime? Explain.

Editor's note: The discussion that follows presents common arguments made in support of this perspective, reinforced by facts, quotes, and examples taken from various sources.

Many Americans not only believe in the right to carry concealed weapons, they believe more people carrying them would make the nation safer. A Gallup poll released in October 2015 found that 56 percent of those surveyed agreed that wider use of concealed carry would actually improve public safety. The poll came in the wake of a deadly shooting on the campus of a community college in Roseburg, Oregon, that left ten dead and nine seriously wounded. The rural campus was a gun-free zone in a state that allows citizens to carry concealed weapons with a permit. Many local residents, joined by gun rights supporters around the

Murder Rates Fall as Number of Concealed Handgun Permits Increases

National murder rates show slight fluctuations from year to year. However, over a period of years those rates have, for the most part, decreased even as the percentage of US adults with permits for concealed carry handguns has increased. Clearly, the right to carry a concealed handgun is a right worth retaining.

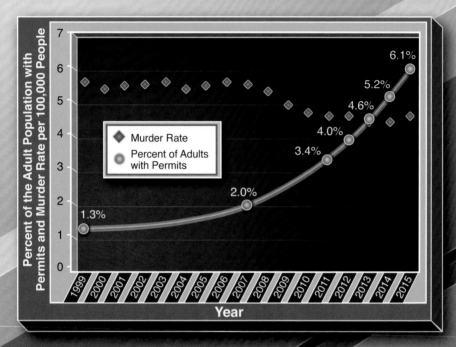

Source: *The Daily Wire*, "Report: Concealed Carry Permit Holders Are the Most Law-Abiding People in the Country," August 10, 2016. www.dailywire.com.

country, felt the college's rules had left students and faculty vulnerable. "Make this a gun-free zone and you paint a target on us," one elderly Oregon man told the *Guardian*. "Criminals will come here because they know no one will damn well shoot back at them."[38]

Gun control activists repeatedly warn that allowing concealed carry will turn American streets into some modern version of the Old West. They envision gunfights breaking out everywhere to settle minor squabbles. But as with so much of their alarmist rhetoric, which aims to strike fear into voters, the reality is quite different. Since 2013, when Illinois passed legislation to allow residents and nonresidents to carry a concealed handgun in public, concealed carry in some form has been legal in all fifty states. Regulations vary in states and cities. Forty-two states require applicants to obtain a permit issued by state or local authorities in order to carry a concealed handgun, while eight others allow concealed carry with no permit. Yet there has been no rash of new gun violence nationwide.

Supporters of firearm rights see the spread of concealed-carry laws as the natural outcome of the Supreme Court's 2008 *Heller* decision, affirming Second Amendment rights for ordinary citizens. "That's kind of the next step in expanding law-abiding gun owners' constitutional right to self-protection," says Jennifer Baker, a spokesperson for the NRA's Institute for Legislative Action. "It's where a lot of states are moving."[39] In fact, some advocates refer to the new policies sweeping the nation as constitutional carry—the right to carry a gun anytime or anyplace, openly or hidden away, without government licensing, registration, or training. Such liberal concealed-carry laws would not be so popular if the majority of voters did not believe they would lead to falling crime rates.

> "More law-abiding citizens own firearms for self-protection, and crime continues to decline."[40]
>
> —Larry Keane, senior vice president and general counsel for the National Shooting Sports Foundation

Criminals Less Likely to Attack

Simple logic suggests that a criminal will think twice before attacking an individual who might be packing a handgun. That moment of hesitation may be crucial in preventing an armed robbery or even a murder. And statistics support this idea. According to the Crime Prevention Research Center, between 2007 and 2015 the number of permits for concealed handguns soared while murder rates actually dropped. During this period concealed-carry permits increased from 4.6 million to more than 12.8 million. At the same time murder rates fell by about 25 percent, from 5.6 to just 4.2 murders per 100,000 people. These numbers are no surprise to gun owners who are exercising their right to concealed carry. "It puts the lie to the myth promulgated by anti-gun individuals that somehow more law-abiding citizens carrying guns will lead to more crime," says Larry Keane, senior vice president and general counsel for the National Shooting Sports Foundation. "In fact, quite the opposite is the case. More law-abiding citizens own firearms for self-protection, and crime continues to decline."[40]

Mass shootings overwhelmingly are perpetrated in places where concealed carry is not allowed—schools, theaters, and shopping malls. Another study by the Crime Prevention Research Center revealed that more than 98 percent of mass shootings from the 1950s to July 2016 occurred in so-called gun-free zones. It is obvious that even mentally unstable shooters and terrorists are careful to choose locations where they are unlikely to encounter anyone with a gun. Many gun rights advocates have speculated that the shooter who murdered a dozen people and wounded fifty-eight others in Aurora, Colorado, in 2012 chose a particular Cinemark movie theater because of its posted no-guns policy. "Gun-free zones are a magnet for those who want to kill many people quickly," declares John R. Lott, a leading expert on gun laws and concealed-carry issues. "Even the most ardent gun control advocate would never put 'Gun-Free Zone' signs on their home."[41] Certainly, a single person with a concealed handgun might have cut short this terrible massacre.

> "Gun-free zones are a magnet for those who want to kill many people quickly. Even the most ardent gun control advocate would never put 'Gun-Free Zone' signs on their home."[41]
>
> —John R. Lott, a leading expert on gun laws and concealed-carry issues

Concealed-Carry Gun Owners Are Law Abiding and Responsible

More than 14.5 million Americans across all fifty states now have permits to carry a concealed handgun. Most people who choose to exercise this right recognize the large responsibility they are assuming. Not only must they learn to shoot and take care of the weapon properly, they must also consider how to avoid conflict and de-escalate dangerous situations if necessary. They must prepare themselves as much as possible to make life-or-death decisions. Oftentimes, they must face criticism or ridicule from those who believe no one but law enforcement officers should be armed. Yet research indicates that individuals who carry a concealed handgun are among the most responsible and law-abiding citizens in the nation.

A recent study suggests that concealed-carry permit holders are convicted of felonies and misdemeanors at a much lower rate than the general population. They even have fewer firearms violations on average than police officers. "Firearms violations among police occur at a rate of 6.9 per 100,000 officers," notes Lott. "For permit holders in Florida, it is only 0.31 per 100,000. Most of these violations were for trivial offenses, such as forgetting to carry one's permit. The data are similar in other states."[42]

Promotes Safety for Women

Concealed carry promises also to be a boon for women's safety. Among law-abiding citizens who carry a concealed weapon are growing numbers of women. From 2012 to 2016, the number of women holding concealed-carry permits grew twice as fast as the number of men with permits. Nationwide the share of permits held by females has grown to 36 percent.

A concealed handgun can make the difference between life and death when a woman is attacked with no one else around. On the night of January 26, 2016, a Kentucky woman found herself being stalked by a stranger as she entered a Louisville shopping mall elevator to the parking lot. When she exited the elevator, the man began chasing her as she ran to her car. The attacker struck the woman and forced his way into her car, brandishing a knife. She was able to pull from her purse a Beretta handgun (for which she had a permit) and shoot the man twice, in the neck and buttocks. Police charged the man with attempted murder and kidnapping. Emily Mattingly, who works in downtown Louisville and often parks in the same garage, said, "I thought it was really empowering for women, in that she could do that, and that she had the confidence to do that."[43] Concealed carry, far from instigating crimes, can be a lifesaver for an innocent female—or anyone else—caught in a deadly situation.

Individuals Should Not Have the Right to Carry a Concealed Handgun

"[With more] people carrying around guns—they're going to be losing them, they're going to be stolen, there are going to be more criminals with guns, and the criminals are more likely to carry guns because they know there are guns out there. For a whole array of reasons, more concealed-gun-carrying outside the home pushes up violent crime."

—John J. Donohue III, Stanford Law School economist and gun control expert

Quoted in Maura Ewing, "Do Right-to-Carry Gun Laws Make States Safer?," *Atlantic*, June 24, 2017. www.theatlantic.com.

Consider these questions as you read:

1. Do you agree with the idea that each state should be able to make its own laws regarding the right to carry a concealed handgun? Why is this important?
2. Which of the arguments against concealed carry presented here do you think is the strongest? Why?
3. How persuasive is the argument that confronting criminals should always be left to police officers? Explain.

Editor's note: The discussion that follows presents common arguments made in support of this perspective, reinforced by facts, quotes, and examples taken from various sources.

The push for legalizing concealed carry in all fifty states is one of the most alarming trends in recent memory. Some members of Congress, egged on by gun rights activists such as the NRA, have even suggested setting up a one-size-fits-all federal concealed-carry law. As *U.S. News & World*

Report notes, this would treat Philadelphia, Mississippi, with its 7,300 people spread out over 100,000 acres (40,469 ha) of farmland, the same as Philadelphia, Pennsylvania, whose more than 1.5 million people are jammed together in an urban environment. "Under a new bill pending in Congress, both Philadelphias would be subject to the exact same gun law," writes reporter Lanae Erickson Hatalsky, "one that allows virtually anyone to carry a loaded concealed gun with them anywhere."[44] This would wipe away the rights of states and localities to craft gun laws that make the most sense for their own citizens and situations.

As it is, concealed-carry laws across the nation are wildly erratic. Some states allow high-risk individuals such as teens, felons with violent crime convictions, and domestic abusers to obtain permits for carrying a loaded concealed handgun. Some states require no concealed-carry permit at all, while others grant permits to out-of-state applicants who would not be eligible in their own state. A nationwide law would saddle the entire country with a policy rife with loopholes and flaccid regulations.

Against this tide of gun rights frenzy, it is vital to stress that no one outside of law enforcement should have the right to carry a concealed weapon. Two centuries of judicial thought on guns considered the right to bear arms as a collective right for state militias, not an individual right for would-be vigilantes. Many towns in the Old West, including Tombstone, Arizona, actually required visitors to stow their six-shooters at the sheriff's office upon arrival. Gun owners today should be required to keep their firearms safely locked away at home. The task of confronting criminals should be left to the police, who are trained for it. Ending concealed carry would also prevent traffic stops or momentary quarrels from escalating into needless tragedies.

Concealed Carry Leads to More Crime and Gun Deaths

The NRA and other gun lobby groups have been misleading the American public for years about concealed carry and falling crime rates. They rely on a controversial and outdated study from 1997 by University of Chicago economists John R. Lott and David Mustard. Lott and Mustard concluded that right-to-carry laws actually reduced crime in a very

Alarming Increase in Concealed-Carry Rights

The spread of concealed-carry rights to all fifty states threatens the health and safety of all Americans. Most states have enacted shall-issue laws in which law enforcement agencies must issue a permit if an applicant completes a background check. Eleven states require no permit for concealed carry whatsoever. The Supreme Court decision that helped make this possible has led to more people packing firearms and threatening violence on US streets.

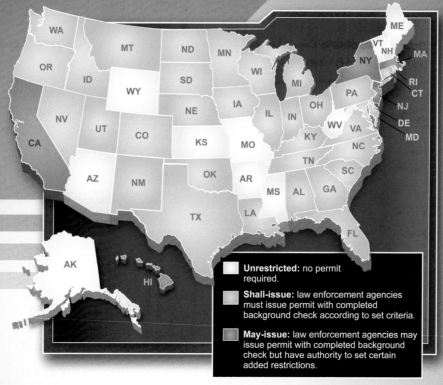

Unrestricted: no permit required.

Shall-issue: law enforcement agencies must issue permit with completed background check according to set criteria.

May-issue: law enforcement agencies may issue permit with completed background check but have authority to set certain added restrictions.

Source: Gun Facts, "Concealed Carry," July 19, 2017. www.gunfacts.info.

cost-effective way. In response, many states began to pass concealed-carry legislation. However, later academic studies debunked the claims made by Lott and Mustard. In fact, a June 2017 study by the nonpartisan National Bureau of Economic Research provided the most decisive evidence yet that crime rises in states where citizens carry concealed handguns. The researchers found that ten years after the right-to-carry laws were adopted in various states, violent crime averaged about 13 percent to

15 percent higher than it was before the laws' enactment. The authors' conclusion was clear-cut: "There is not even the slightest hint in the data that [these] laws reduce violent crime."[45]

The usefulness of concealed carry for self-defense is also questionable. A 2015 report by the Violence Policy Center consulted federal data and news accounts over several years to show that private citizens rarely use guns to kill a criminal or stop a crime. In 722 deaths from concealed-carry shootings in 36 states and the District of Columbia, only 16 cases were ruled to be lawful self-defense. "The NRA has staked its entire agenda on the claim that guns are necessary for self-defense, but this gun industry propaganda has no basis in fact," says Violence Policy Center executive director Josh Sugarmann. "Guns are far more likely to be used in a homicide than in a justifiable homicide by a private citizen. In fact, a gun is far more likely to be stolen than used in self-defense."[46]

States often are leery about releasing data related to concealed-carry incidents, and the NRA's congressional allies also are reluctant to break down the figures for public consumption. However, almost thirty-eight hundred people died from accidental shootings from 2005 to 2010, according to the Law Center to Prevent Gun Violence. Most of these people were under twenty-five years of age. The Gun Violence Archive, which tracks shooting incidents in the United States, says accidental gun deaths among small children have spiked since 2015. Common sense suggests a significant number of these deaths were connected to guns left loaded and unsecured due to a concealed-carry permit.

> "Guns are far more likely to be used in a homicide than in a justifiable homicide by a private citizen. In fact, a gun is far more likely to be stolen than used in self-defense."[46]
>
> —Josh Sugarmann, executive director of the Violence Policy Center

Disputes Become Deadly

Letting people carry handguns in public greatly increases the likelihood that some small dispute will blow up into a shooting. By nature, those drawn to concealed carry are self-assertive—and some would say irresponsibly aggressive. This attitude can lead to violence. "It is hard to find a more zealous group than conceal carriers," says investigative reporter Martha Rosenberg. "They see 'bad guys' everywhere, have a high fear level and flatter themselves that they are keeping themselves and others safe."[47]

Rosenberg points to George Zimmerman, a Florida man with a concealed-carry permit who ended up killing Trayvon Martin, a young black man, in a 2012 case that divided the nation. After a series of break-ins in his neighborhood, Zimmerman was on the lookout one evening for intruders. He spotted Martin, who was on foot and heading to his girlfriend's house. Zimmerman called 911 to report a suspicious person and was told by police not to approach the person. He disobeyed this order and confronted Martin, which led to a fight. In the struggle, Zimmerman pulled a handgun from his holster and shot Martin at close range. Zimmerman eventually was tried on second-degree murder charges and found not guilty.

> "It seems that every week I read about someone using his or her handgun in a situation where he or she would better have backed away and allowed sworn officers to take over."[49]
>
> —Rick Sapp, spokesperson for the United States Concealed Carry Association

The incident led to a heated national debate on concealed-carry laws. Many observers felt it was Zimmerman's possession of a handgun that caused an ugly confrontation to end in a needless killing. "The fact is that the exact scenarios that [gun rights] advocacy groups said would never happen do happen," says Josh Sugarmann, "that concealed carry handgun holders do kill and not just in self-defense situations, but in road rage, domestic shootings, arguments, and bar fights."[48]

Leave Crime Control to Law Enforcement

Not only do gun owners with concealed-carry permits tempt escalations of violence, they often think of themselves as unofficial police officers. The truth is that they lack anything close to the training and expertise to use their firearms wisely in a dangerous situation. Rick Sapp, spokesperson for the United States Concealed Carry Association, acknowledges the problem. A gun owner may have a permit and have received some training. "But you are not a cop," says Sapp. "Cops have hundreds of hours, perhaps thousands in a lifetime, of serve-and-protect. You are not Captain America. It seems that every week I read about someone using his or her handgun in a situation where he or she would better have backed away and allowed sworn officers to take over."[49]

The truth is that police officers face untold headaches from concealed-carry zealots. A simple traffic stop can become a lethal confrontation when the driver does not carefully follow protocol in revealing his or her possession of a handgun. Would-be vigilantes with firearms can complicate the police pursuit of criminals. The best solution is to repeal concealed-carry laws and let trained law enforcement officers do their jobs.

Source Notes

Overview: Gun Control

1. Quoted in Stephen Dinan and Seth McLaughlin, "Capitol Police Heroes Used Guns to Prevent Massacre on Ballfield," *Washington Times,* June 14, 2017. www.washingtontimes.com.
2. Quoted in Liz Stark, "Where Does GOP Baseball Shooting Leave the Gun Control Debate?," CNN, June 16, 2017. www.cnn.com.
3. Thomas Sowell, "The Gun-Control Farce," *National Review*, June 21, 2016. www.nationalreview.com.
4. Quoted in National Archives, "The Bill of Rights: A Transcription," June 26, 2017. www.archives.gov.
5. Jeffrey Toobin, "So You Think You Know the Second Amendment?," *New Yorker*, December 17, 2012. www.newyorker.com.
6. *District of Columbia v. Heller*, 554 U.S. 570 (2008).

Chapter One: Do Gun Control Laws Reduce Gun-Related Deaths?

7. Quoted in Lauren Carroll, "Obama: More Gun Laws Means Fewer Gun Deaths," PolitiFact, October 6, 2015. www.politifact.com.
8. Quoted in Douglas Hanks, "Orlando Gunman's Weapon of Choice: Legal in Florida, Banned in New York," *Miami Herald*, June 13, 2016. www.miamiherald.com.
9. Quoted in Anthony Faiola, "After Shooting Tragedies, Britain Went After Guns," *Washington Post*, February 1, 2013. www.washington post.com.
10. John Howard, "Australia Banned Assault Weapons. America Can, Too," *New York Times*, January 19, 2013. www.nytimes.com.
11. Quoted in Laura Smith-Spark, "This Is What Happened When Australia Introduced Tight Gun Controls," CNN, June 19, 2015. www.cnn.com.
12. Quoted in Jacob Davidson, "A Criminologist's Case Against Gun Control," *Time*, December 1, 2015. http://time.com.

13. Ben Domenech, "The Truth About Mass Shootings and Gun Control," *Commentary*, February 1, 2013. www.commentarymagazine.com.

14. Quoted in Becky Bowers, "Marco Rubio Says After D.C. Passed Gun Laws, 'Violence Skyrocketed,'" PolitiFact, January 28, 2013. www.politifact.com.

15. Quoted in Stephen Gutowski, "Study Finds That Chicago Criminals Get Guns from Friends, Family," *Washington Free Beacon*, September 3, 2015. http://freebeacon.com.

16. Quoted in Gutowski, "Study Finds That Chicago Criminals Get Guns from Friends, Family."

Chapter Two: Should Background Checks for Gun Buyers Be Expanded?

17. Quoted in Greg Sargent, "Conservative Pro-Gun Senator Demolishes Arguments Against Background Checks," *Washington Post*, April 12, 2013. www.washingtonpost.com.

18. Gun Control Act of 1968, Public Law 90-618 (1968).

19. Quoted in Michael Cooper et al., "Loopholes in Gun Laws Allow Buyers to Skirt Checks," *New York Times*, April 10, 2013. www.nytimes.com.

20. Quoted in Ben Casselman, "Where Background Checks Work," FiveThirtyEight, July 13, 2016. https://fivethirtyeight.com.

21. Quoted in Victor Luckerson, "Read Barack Obama's Speech on New Gun Control Measures," *Time*, January 5, 2016. http://time.com.

22. Quoted in Michael S. Schmidt, "Both Sides in Gun Debate Agree: Punish Background-Check Liars," *New York Times*, January 13, 2013. www.nytimes.

23. Quoted in Fox News, "Universal Background Checks Do Little to Stop Mass Shootings, Study Finds," January 5, 2016. www.foxnews.com.

24. Law Center to Prevent Gun Violence, "Waiting Periods," 2017. http://smartgunlaws.org.

25. Beth Baumann, "Here Is Some Good News for California Gun Owners," TheBlaze, March 28, 2016. www.theblaze.com.

26. Quoted in Chris Good, "The Case Against Gun Background Checks," ABC News, April 10, 2013. http://abcnews.go.com.

Chapter Three: Should Military-Style Assault Weapons Be Banned?

27. Quoted in Chris Mejaski, "Celebrities React to Mass Shooting at Orlando Gay Club," etalk, June 13, 2016. www.etalk.ca.

28. Quoted in James Gherardi, "The Weapon Used in Orlando and Almost Every Mass Shooting in the U.S. is the AR-15 Semi-Automatic Rifle," Fox59, June 14, 2016. http://fox59.com.

29. Quoted in Douglas Ernst, "Alan Grayson Claims AR-15s Can Fire '700 Rounds in a Minute' After Orlando Attack," *Washington Times*, June 13, 2016. www.washingtontimes.com.

30. NRA-ILA, "Ten Reasons Why States Should Reject 'Assault Weapon' and 'Large' Magazine Bans," June 17, 2014. www.nraila.org.

31. Dovid Bendory, "'High Cap Freedom': Five Reasons Why You Should Want High Capacity Magazines," Jews for the Preservation of Firearms Ownership, 2011. http://jpfo.org.

32. Andrew Cline, "America Is Awash in Guns, and Crime Is at Record Lows," *Federalist*, June 22, 2016. http://thefederalist.com.

33. Quoted in Andrew Buncombe, "Orlando Shooting: Campaigners Demand Ban of AR-15 Rifle—'the Gold Standard for Mass Murder of Innocent Civilians,'" *Independent* (London), June 13, 2016. www .independent.co.uk.

34. Sarah Zhang, "What an AR-15 Can Do to the Human Body," *Wired*, June 17, 2016. www.wired.com.

35. Bernie Horn, "Can We Do Anything About Murderous Assault Weapons?," Common Dreams, June 14, 2016. www.common dreams.org.

36. "Large Capacity Magazines," Law Center to Prevent Gun Violence, 2017. http://smartgunlaws.org.

37. Quoted in Catherine E. Shoichet, "Mexico's President to U.S.: 'No More Weapons,'" CNN, February 17, 2012. www.cnn.com.

Chapter Four: Should Individuals Have the Right to Carry a Concealed Handgun?

38. Quoted in Rory Carroll, "Oregon College Shooting Is All the More Reason to Carry Guns, Say Local Residents," *Guardian* (Manchester), October 2, 2015. www.theguardian.com.

39. Quoted in Katie Zezima, "More States Are Allowing People to Carry Concealed Handguns Without a Permit," *Washington Post*, February 24, 2017. www.washingtonpost.com.

40. Quoted in Kellan Howell, "Murder Rates Drop as Concealed Carry Permits Soar: Report," *Washington Times*, July 14, 2015. www.washingtontimes.com.

41. John R. Lott, "Did Colorado Shooter Single Out Cinemark Theater Because It Banned Guns?," Fox News, September 10, 2012. www.foxnews.com.

42. John R. Lott, "Guns and the *New York Times*: Why Shouldn't Americans Be Able to Defend Themselves?," Fox News, February 24, 2015. www.foxnews.com.

43. Quoted in Christina Mora, "LMPD: Woman Shoots Man Trying to Rob Her Downtown," WLKY, January 27, 2016. www.wlky.com.

44. Lanae Erickson Hatalsky and Sarah Trumble, "A Gun Law That Hurts Everyone," *U.S. News & World Report*, January 25, 2017. www.usnews.com.

45. Quoted in Maura Ewing, "Do Right-to-Carry Gun Laws Make States Safer?," *Atlantic*, June 24, 2017. www.theatlantic.com.

46. Quoted in Violence Policy Center, "Self-Defense Gun Use Is Rare, Study Finds," June 17, 2015. www.vpc.org.

47. Martha Rosenberg, "Think Concealed Carry Makes You Safe? Think Again!," *Huffington Post*, June 26, 2013. www.huffingtonpost.com.

48. Quoted in Patrik Jonsson, "Trayvon Martin Shooting: A Turning Point in Gun Rights Debate?," *Christian Science Monitor*, April 19, 2012. www.csmonitor.com.

49. Rick Sapp, "You Are Not a Cop," United States Concealed Carry Association, March 18, 2016. www.usconcealedcarry.com.

Gun Control Facts

Concealed Carry

- A 2017 study by the Crime Prevention Research Center found that there were currently more than 16.3 million handgun permits in the United States; 2016 also saw the largest increase ever in the number of new permits issued.
- In Alaska, Arizona, Vermont, and Wyoming, a person may carry a concealed handgun without any sort of permit. Georgia and Maryland are among the states that do not require firearms training before receiving a permit for concealed carry.
- Since Alaska enacted so-called constitutional carry—carrying a handgun without a permit—the number of handgun murders in the state has declined. In the fourteen years since its passage, handgun murders in Alaska have also declined as a percentage of total murders.
- Eugene Volokh, a blogger for the *Washington Post*, has found at least eight cases since 2007 in which an armed civilian has prevented a mass shooting. At the same time, the Violence Policy Center has documented twenty-nine mass shootings (with three or more victims) since 2007 in which the shooter had a permit for concealed carry.

Gun Manufacturing and Ownership

- According to the Bureau of Alcohol, Tobacco, Firearms and Explosives, the number of guns manufactured in the United States almost doubled in the first few years of the Obama administration. The number went from nearly 5.5 million in 2010 to nearly 10.9 million in 2013.
- In 2016 *USA Today* reported that 3 percent of Americans own half the guns in the country. The percentage of American households with guns has actually decreased substantially, from about 46 percent in 1975 to about 32 percent in 2015.

- The Switzerland-based Small Arms Survey lists the top five countries for gun ownership per capita as follows: the United States, Yemen, Switzerland, Finland, and Serbia. The United States is estimated to have 88.8 guns for every 100 residents, the highest rate in the world.
- A 2017 survey by the Pew Research Center found that the area of the United States where gun ownership is least common is the Northeast. Only 16 percent of the people surveyed there identified themselves as gun owners.
- According to the Pew survey, gun ownership rates are roughly equal in other areas of the country. The South has 36 percent gun owners, the Midwest has 32 percent, and the West has 31 percent.

Background Checks and Waiting Periods

- The FBI reports that its National Instant Criminal Background Check System issued 1,393,729 denials between 1998 and 2016. The total number of denials in 2016 was 120,497.
- The number of federal background checks grew from about 8.5 million in 2000 to more than 27.5 million in 2016.
- Federal law allows a gun dealer to deliver a firearm to a buyer the instant a background check is completed. This process usually takes only a few minutes. If the background check has not been completed in three business days, the gun dealer can go ahead and deliver the firearm. Federal officials estimate more than three thousand ineligible buyers each year obtain firearms through this loophole.
- California, Rhode Island, and the District of Columbia require a statutory waiting period on every firearm purchase. In California and the District of Columbia, the period is ten days. Rhode Island has a waiting period of seven days.

Other Gun Control Facts

- The *New York Times* reports that about 60 percent of people who are killed by guns die by suicide. The Brady Campaign to Prevent Gun Violence claims there are more than fifty gun suicides each day and about twenty thousand each year.

- Studies show that mental illness is not a significant factor in gun violence. Columbia University's Paul Appelbaum and Duke University's Jeffrey Swanson found that only about 3 percent to 5 percent of violent acts are the result of serious mental illness, and most are not committed with guns.
- According to a 2016 study by the *American Journal of Medicine*, Americans are ten times more likely to die from gun violence than people in other developed nations. The rate of gun homicides per 100,000 people in the United States is 3.6. This compares to 0.2 for Australia, 0.5 for Canada, 0.1 for Germany, and 0.2 for France.
- A 2016 survey of the National Association of Chiefs of Police found that 86.4 percent of twenty thousand police chiefs and sheriffs are in favor of concealed carry and opposed to more gun control laws. From 2013 to 2015 the rate of police killings went up in the six states plus the District of Columbia where concealed carry was banned.
- Some gun control advocates contend that it is easy to convert an assault rifle like the AR-15 to a fully automatic firearm. However, gun experts insist that the AR-15 cannot be converted so easily and that it tends to jam if fired too rapidly. Converting a firearm into an automatic weapon is also illegal.
- A study by Northeastern University found that only about one-fourth of mass shootings were committed with an assault weapon like an AR-15. About 50 percent of such shootings were actually committed with handguns.

Related Organizations and Websites

Brady Center to Prevent Gun Violence
840 First St. NE, Suite 400
Washington, DC 20002
e-mail: policy@bradymail.org
website: www.bradycampaign.org

The Brady Center to Prevent Gun Violence is a nonprofit organization that advocates for gun control initiatives such as expanded background checks and educates the public about the real dangers of guns in the home. The mission of the Brady Center is to create a safer America by cutting gun deaths in half by 2025.

Brookings Institution
1775 Massachusetts Ave. NW
Washington, DC 20036
e-mail: communications@brookings.edu
website: www.brookings.edu

The Brookings Institution is a nonprofit public policy organization that does independent research and offers innovative, practical recommendations on vital issues of the day, including gun control policy. The Brookings Institution is consistently rated one of the most influential think tanks in the United States.

Cato Institute
1000 Massachusetts Ave. NW
Washington, DC 20001
e-mail: information@cato.org
website: www.cato.org

The Cato Institute is a public policy research organization—a think tank—dedicated to the principles of individual liberty, limited government, free markets, and peace. Its scholars and analysts conduct independent, nonpartisan research on a wide range of policy issues, including gun control and gun rights.

Center for American Progress (CAP)
1333 H St. NW
Washington, DC 20005
website: www.americanprogress.org

CAP is an educational institute that promotes progressive ideas to improve the lives of Americans. It is a supporter of gun control initiatives and works to end gun violence.

Heritage Foundation
214 Massachusetts Ave. NE
Washington, DC 20002
e-mail: info@heritage.org
website: www.heritage.org

The Heritage Foundation is a research and educational institution whose mission is to formulate and promote conservative public policies based on the principles of free enterprise, limited government, individual freedom, traditional American values, and a strong national defense. These policies include gun rights according to the Second Amendment.

Law Center to Prevent Gun Violence
268 Bush St. #555
San Francisco, CA 94104
e-mail: info@smartgunlaws.org
website: http://smartgunlaws.org

The Law Center to Prevent Gun Violence is the premier resource for legal expertise and information regarding state and federal firearms laws. It works with lawmakers and advocates to create and promote legislation that will reduce gun violence and save lives.

National Rifle Association (NRA)
11250 Waples Mill Rd.
Fairfax, VA 22030
website: https://home.nra.org

The NRA is America's foremost defender of Second Amendment rights and the world's premier firearms education organization. It is also a major political force in legislative battles over gun control.

United States Concealed Carry Association (USCCA)
Delta Defense, LLC
1000 Freedom Way
West Bend, WI 53095
website: www.usconcealedcarry.com

The USCCA is an organization devoted to informing Americans about their rights regarding self-defense and carrying a concealed weapon.

Violence Policy Center (VPC)
1025 Connecticut Ave. NW, Suite 1210
Washington, DC 20036
website: www.vpc.org

The VPC is a group that works to stop gun deaths and injuries through research, education, advocacy, and collaboration. The VPC seeks to inform the public about the impact of gun violence on their daily lives and exposes the lobbying activities of the firearms industry and gun lobby.

For Further Research

Books

Philip J. Cook and Kristin A. Goss, *The Gun Debate: What Everyone Needs to Know*. New York: Oxford University Press, 2014.

Dennis A. Henigan, *"Guns Don't Kill People, People Kill People": And Other Myths About Guns and Gun Control*. Boston: Beacon, 2016.

John R. Lott Jr., *The War on Guns: Arming Yourself Against Gun Control Lies*. Washington, DC: Regnery, 2016.

Michael Waldman, *The Second Amendment: A Biography*. New York: Simon & Schuster, 2014.

Adam Winkler, *Gunfight: The Battle over the Right to Bear Arms in America*. New York: Norton, 2013.

Internet Sources

Ben Casselman, "Where Background Checks Work," FiveThirtyEight, July 13, 2016. https://fivethirtyeight.com/features/background-checks/.

Seth Cline, "The Gun Control Debate, in Plain English," *U.S. News & World Report*, December 18, 2012. www.usnews.com/news/articles /2012/12/18/the-gun-control-debate-in-plain-english.

Maura Ewing, "Do Right-to-Carry Gun Laws Make States Safer?," *Atlantic*, June 24, 2017. www.theatlantic.com/politics/archive/2017/06/right -to-carry-gun-violence/531297/.

Bernie Horn, "Can We Do Anything About Murderous Assault Weapons?," *Common Dreams,* June 14, 2016. www.commondreams.org/views /2016/06/14/can-we-do-anything-about-murderous-assault-weapons.

Laws.com, "A Full Overview of Gun Control," 2017. http://gun.laws
.com/gun-control.

Robert Perez-Pena, "Gun Control Explained," *New York Times*, October 7, 2015. www.nytimes.com/interactive/2015/10/07/us/gun-control
-explained.html?mcubz=1.

Katie Zezima, "More States Are Allowing People to Carry Concealed Handguns Without a Permit," *Washington Post*, February 24, 2017. www.washingtonpost.com/news/post-nation/wp/2017/02/24/more
-states-are-allowing-people-to-carry-concealed-handguns-without-a
-permit/?utm_term=.3b9587fa2375.

Sarah Zhang, "What an AR-15 Can Do to the Human Body," *Wired*, June 17, 2016. www.wired.com/2016/06/ar-15-can-human-body/.

Index

About the Author

John Allen is a writer living in Oklahoma City.